Get the SCOOP on Animal POOP!

Get the
SCOOP
on
Animal
POOP!

Dawn Cusick

From Lions to Tapeworms

251 Cool Facts about Scat, Frass, Dung, and More!

imagine!
Publishing

to Eric Isselée,
a most extraordinary
animal photographer

An Imagine Book
Published by Charlesbridge
85 Main Street
Watertown, MA 02472
(617) 926-0329
www.charlesbridge.com

Library of Congress Cataloging-in-Publication Data is
available upon request.

ISBN: 978-1-62354-014-2

Printed in China. Manufactured in October, 2014.

10 9 8 7 6 5 4 3 2

Display type and text type set in Geometric Slab and Magelsom.

Jacket and Type Design: Celia Naranjo
Editorial Assistance: Catherine Ham and Katy Nelson
Produced by EarlyLight Books

For information about custom editions, special sales,
premium and corporate purchases, please contact
Charlesbridge Publishing at specialsales@charlesbridge.com

CONTENTS

INTRODUCTION

You have a very important decision to make. Really. No kidding.

   Here it is in one simple sentence: How will you deal with the adults in your life when they see this book?

   Of course, you can always say nothing. Just hide the book in your backpack or your sock drawer and make sure they don't catch you grinning after you've been looking at it.

Another option is to just laugh at the grown-ups' disgust and let them think you're just a silly kid who likes potty humor. Let them think the artistic swirl of spicy brown mustard to the right is really a photograph of poop.

There's a third tactic you can take, but it's not for the faint of heart. You can try—repeat, TRY— educating adults. Explain that there's real science in this book, that animal poop is part of food chains around the world, and that sometimes it's the backbone of an entire ecosystem or a habitat for hundreds of species.

If you have some success, you can try teaching them how animals use feces to send chemical messages or how they use poop to trick predators and prey. Be prepared for skepticism and be ready to show them your favorite pictures and cool facts.

Whichever decision you make, make sure you have fun getting the scoop on animal poop!

There are dozens of words used to describe the body waste of animals. Some words are scientific and precise, referring only to specific animals, while some words are silly and make us laugh. Other words will make adult eyebrows go up and get you in trouble, but we won't use those here!

Bat Guano

FECES: Waste material expelled from an animal's body.

FECAL MATTER: Small or large amounts of feces.

EXCREMENT: Feces.

FECAL SAC: A gelatin-like sac that contains a baby bird's feces; parent birds remove or eat the sacs to keep their nests clean.

FRASS: The waste material of insects.

DUNG: Feces; sometimes used to describe feces released in large piles.

SCAT: Feces. Many carnivores use scat as a communication tool.

DROPPINGS: Feces; sometimes used to describe feces released in small pieces; also used to describe the feces of many birds.

GUANO: The feces of seabirds and bats. Guano is in high demand now as an organic fertilizer.

SPRAINT: Otter feces.

DEFECATE: The act of releasing feces.

COPROLOGY: The study of feces; also called SCATOLOGY.

LANGUAGE!

Bluebird Droppings

Alpaca Droppings

Buffalo Dung

Bear Scat

Termite Frass

Who Needs A Frisbee?

The flat, round shape of dried cow dung has inspired many nicknames, including cow patty, cow pie, meadow muffin, and cow chip. Dried cow dung is also used as Frisbees in "Cow Chip Throwing" competitions at state fairs. Let's hope they wash their hands before they eat cotton candy!

ALL ANIMALS POOP

All organisms in the Animal Kingdom ingest their food—that's what makes them an animal. (Fungi absorb their food, and plants make their own.) Every animal that ingests food, though, must also remove the parts that it cannot use as waste.

Tails up!

Many large animals, including the giraffe, have surprisingly small fecal pellets.

Bombs Away!

Compared to giraffes, elephants release their feces in much larger pieces!

Many smaller animals find their food in elephant dung. See page 17 for some cool examples.

Hold that Thought!

What can you and I do that a cow cannot? Any ideas?

You and I have large intestines (see page 14 for more info), a place in our bodies that works to store feces until we're ready to expel them. If you had a cow in your classroom, he could not "hold it" until the next restroom break. When a cow's feces is made, out it comes!

ALL ANIMALS POOP

Many advanced animals have an alimentary canal, a long tube that starts with the mouth and ends with the anus, where food is digested and waste is released. The illustration to the left shows the alimentary canal in a human. The bulging area at the top is the stomach, where food is mixed and broken down. The winding tube in the center is the small intestine, where nutrients are absorbed into the bloodstream. The larger, gold part of the tube is the large intestine, where feces is stored until it's expressed through the anus at the end of the colon.

No Alimentary Canals in These Guys . . .

Nematodes, also known as roundworms, have special cells that remove waste from their bodies. Other types of primitive animals, including the flatworms and the rotifers, also have waste-removing cells.

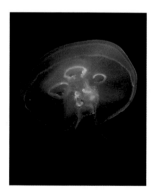

Jellyfish have incomplete digestive systems, which means their waste comes out the same place their food goes in. Think about that for a few minutes!

In One End and out the Other!

Grasshoppers, snails, and many other types of animals have complete digestive systems (like people do), which means that food goes in one end of the body through the mouth and waste comes out through the anus at the other end.

Brown AND White?

Reptiles and birds have complete digestive systems, just like we do. They only have one body opening for waste, which is called a cloaca, so when you come across their poo, you sometimes see solid white urine next to their feces.

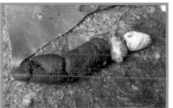

Yes, Fish Poop, Too!

Fish need to remove wastes from their bodies, too. See pages 46-51 to learn more.

Pellets or Piles?

Shapes and sizes of animal poop vary a lot and depend on how long feces stays in the body, what foods the animal eats, and many other factors. See page 70 to learn more.

WHAT'S IN THERE?

Believe it or not, an animal's waste material is an ecosystem. Just like the ecosystems you've probably studied in school, there are living things (biotic) and nonliving things (abiotic) in animal poop, even after it leaves an animal's body.

Run for Your Life!

When biologists looked at lion feces under microscopes, they were surprised to find chimpanzee fur. Generally, the fur of prey animals is not broken down in the predators' digestive systems, and passes through their bodies in their poop.

Look Close

Animal feces can contain partially digested foods. If you look carefully at this elephant dung, you can see undigested grass.

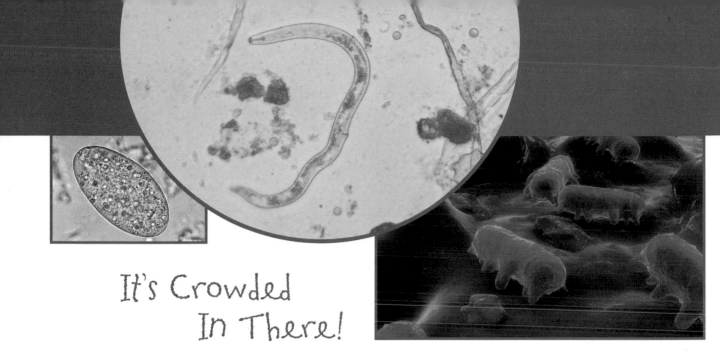

It's Crowded In There!

Animal poop contains millions of bacteria. Some types, such as the *Salmonella* shown here (above right), can make people sick if they are accidentally eaten. Most feces also contains parasites (above center) and parasite eggs (above left). Think about this the next time someone reminds you to wash your hands after using the restroom!

Dinner Time

Some insect-eating animals look through animal poop, searching for insects. Shown here, a vervet monkey (left) and a ground hornbill (below left) forage in feces for food.

Egg Nest

Some insects lay their eggs in fresh feces. The May bug in this photo is a newly hatched larva.

PEE-YEW

When we feed ourselves, we also feed the bacteria living in our intestines. These bacteria release hydrogen sulfide, the stinky part of gas, as they break down molecules left-over from the red meat we eat. People who do not eat meat reportedly have less gas and fewer foul-smelling feces. So, are you off the flatulence hook if you're a vegetarian? Probably not. Many vegetables and bran products cause gas, too!

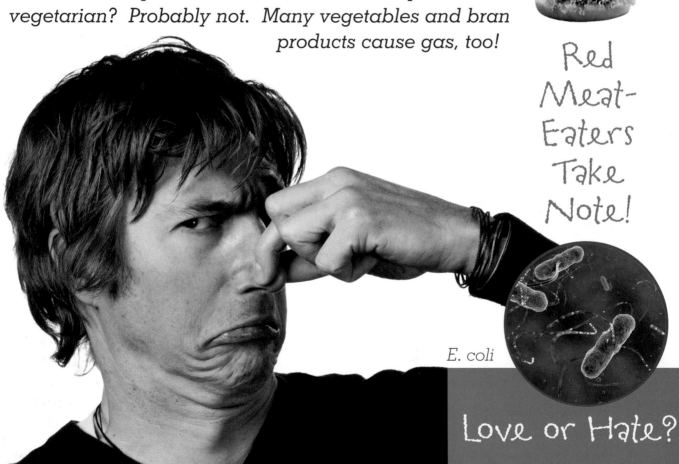

Red Meat-Eaters Take Note!

E. coli

Love or Hate?

Should we hate these gas-making bacteria? No, no, no! Even though they can cause stinky situations, these bacteria also help us get nutrients from our food.

Carnivore Tricks of The Trade

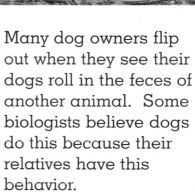

Catching dinner can be hard work for a carnivore. Most prey animals have a strong sense of smell, and know to run away when danger is near. To trick their prey, predators such as wolves (above), jackals (below), and lions roll in the dung of a plant-eater before they go hunting.

Herbivores, such as the antelope at right, sniff the feces they find in their territories. If they smell the feces of a predator, they leave.

Jackal Guarding Elephant Dung

Many dog owners flip out when they see their dogs roll in the feces of another animal. Some biologists believe dogs do this because their relatives have this behavior.

If you put 50 kids on one end of a room and a large table filled with donuts, cakes, and candy on the other end, where would you find most of the kids in ten minutes? When you think of where food is digested in animals, it's not surprising that we find so many parasites in the small and large intestines, and also in feces. For parasites, the intestines are like an all-you-can-eat buffet table filled with their favorite treats!

Zombie Ants? Really?

WHAT on earth is wrong with this ant? See the top of the next page to find out.

"Shouldn't You Be Running For Your Life?"

Toxoplasma gondii, a parasite that lives in feline intestines, moves out of cats in their feces and then infects rats and mice. The parasite's life cycle is completed when a cat eats a rat or mouse. Scientists were amazed to find out that rats infected with toxoplasmosis were less afraid of cats! People can also be infected with toxoplasmosis.

Yes, Zombie Ants!

Believe it or not, the ant below left was infected with a fungal parasite when it ate bird droppings. The parasite causes a growth on the ant's head, which, to a bird flying overhead, looks like a tasty berry. When the bird eats the ant, it is infected with the parasite and the life cycle is completed. Infected ants are called zombie ants because they stop hiding and put themselves in the path of predators.

As crazy as the idea of zombie ants sounds, biologists have found many examples of parasites changing the behavior of their hosts in ways that help the parasite reproduce more. The Cuban postage stamps above were designed to teach people about parasites such as tapeworms that can cause human diseases. The illustrations in each corner show the parasite's life cycle.

Meet the Pinworms

Pinworms are small worms that live in human intestines. Females lay their eggs near the anal opening of young children in a sticky, itchy liquid. When children scratch the itch, the eggs move from their hands to their mouths and later to their intestines, which completes the parasite's life cycle.

SNACK ATTACK

It sounds gross to us, but animals eat poop for good reasons. Sometimes the feces has a nutrient in it that an animal's body needs. Other times, feces is a food source an animal can't afford to ignore because competition for food is very tough.

Life Is Sweet!

Aphid insects poop a sweet, liquid waste called honeydew. Some species of ants protect aphids from predators in return for honeydew snacks. The photo shows an ant about to feed on honeydew.

Picky Eaters?

Many types of ants get nutrients from bird droppings, which are a mix of feces and urine.

Wipe Your Feet, Please

Flying takes a lot of energy, so poop is a valuable food for flies. As they feed, fecal matter gets on the bottoms of their feet. When flies move on to their next feeding site—which might well be your potato salad—their dirty feet transfer small bits of poop, which can cause diseases in humans.

Ewwwww . . .

COPROPHAGIA:
Feces eating.

The word comes from two Greek words, *phagein*, which means to eat, and *kopros*, which means feces.

Some animals only eat poop from another species, while other animals will eat any poop they find.

Again:
Ewwwww . . .

Gorillas and some other primates occasionally eat their own feces. Biologists aren't sure why they do this, but it may be to get extra vitamins from foods not completely digested the first time.

SNACK ATTACK

Rat Buffet!

Rats and mice often eat dog feces to get small pieces of undigested food.

Good Reasons!

Young pandas, rhinos, and some other herbivore mammals need a special type of bacteria in their intestines to help them digest plants. To get these bacteria into their bodies, they eat the poop of their parents or other members of their species!

SNACK ATTACK

ABOVE AND FAR RIGHT: By eating the feces of older elephants, young elephants obtain the microbes they need to digest plants. Young termites also eat the feces of adults to get digestion microbes.

RIGHT: When not eating grasses or roots, warthogs eat the feces of large herbivores to get partially digested nutrients.

Home, Sweet Home

If the woman standing closest to this termite mound is 5 feet tall, can you estimate how tall this termite mound is? This mound is in a public park in Australia.

Termite mounds are made from termite feces and saliva, chewed wood, and mud. Several million termites can live in each colony.

LIGHTEN THE LOAD

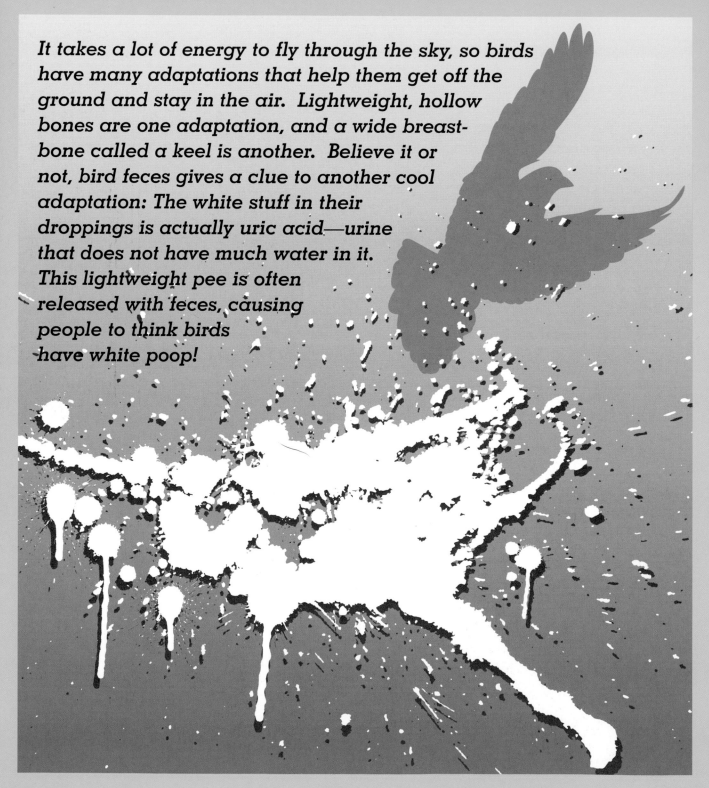

It takes a lot of energy to fly through the sky, so birds have many adaptations that help them get off the ground and stay in the air. Lightweight, hollow bones are one adaptation, and a wide breast-bone called a keel is another. Believe it or not, bird feces gives a clue to another cool adaptation: The white stuff in their droppings is actually uric acid—urine that does not have much water in it. This lightweight pee is often released with feces, causing people to think birds have white poop!

Splat Attack!

The amount of splatter a bird's feces creates is a matter of simple physics and depends on three questions: How far is the feces falling? (In other words, how high up in the air is the bird when it defecates?) How much does the feces weigh? And how hard is the surface it lands on?

Don't Look Up!

Poop Detectives

Some biologists collect samples of bird droppings and bring them back to their labs. They test the poop for viruses and bacteria that can make people sick.

THE POWER OF POO!

Homemade Bug Spray Saves The Day (and the Chicks!)

Many ground-nesting birds such as the blue-footed boobie (above left and above) and the penguin (left) make "poop rings" around their nests. Some biologists believe the birds' feces keeps insects away from their eggs.

Look at Me!

For a long time, biologists did not understand why Egyptian vultures ate the dung of goats, cows, and sheep. Vultures, after all, are known for eating dead animals, which is called carrion. It turns out the vultures eat feces to find carotenoids, a type of pigment that adds color to root vegetables. These pigments make the birds' faces bright yellow, which may advertise their strength to other birds.

Poopy Nickname: In Spain, Egyptian vultures are called *churretero* and *moniguero*, which both translate to poop-eater!

After-Dinner Clean-Up!

Your mom probably asks you to wash your hands before dinner, right? Well, if you were a turkey vulture (right), you would need to wash up AFTER dinner! Turkey vultures stand in rotting flesh while they eat. To kill germs and bacteria on their legs, turkey vultures defecate on them-selves. Their feces contains special anti-bacterial chemicals which kill germs just like your mom's hand soap does.

PLANTS & POOP

Everyone knows how important plants are to the world's ecosystems, but did you know how important animal poop is to plants? Check out the following cool examples.

Take Me Away!

There are about 1,000 species of bats, and many of them eat insects. Some bats eat fruits, though, and help plants by carrying fruit seeds to areas where there may be less competition for sun and soil. By the time the seeds move through a bat's digestive system and out of its feces, the bat may be far away from the parent plant's original location.

Free Fertilizer!

Earthworms help plants in several ways. While traveling underground, earthworms eat soil, moving nitrogen and nutrients to the surface for plants to use. Their feces also acts as fertilizer.

Scarification Isn't So Scary . . .

Some plant seeds have an extra-thick coating that keeps them dormant. The seeds will not germinate unless this outer coating is scratched or scarred. When birds eat seeds, they get some nutrients from the seed's outer surface, which causes scarring. When the seeds pass through the birds' digestive tract, they exit ready to germinate.

Cream & Sugar?

The most expensive coffee in the world may be kopi luwak. This coffee is made from coffee beans that have been eaten and scarred by the palm civet, a relative of the mongoose. The scarred beans are collected from the animals' feces!

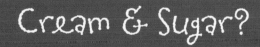

POOP PRETENDERS

Some animals and plants hide from predators by disguising themselves as feces. So why don't feces-eating animals such as the ants on page 22 eat them? Because ants find poop by the way it smells, not by the way it looks. Birds, on the other hand, use their eyesight to find food and don't eat poop, so the caterpillars' camouflage trick works well.

Who Goes There?

The dung spider (above) was named after dung because it looks like a pile of poop when it folds up its legs!

Who Stepped In Dog Doo?

Ginkgo trees are often called living fossils because they are some of the oldest trees on Earth and they have few living relatives.

How has the ginkgo managed to outlive so many other trees? Scientists often mention the ginkgo's ability to survive droughts and other tough conditions as explanations.

The berries of ginkgo trees may also help explain their living fossil status. When squeezed or stepped on, these berries smell like dog feces!

Why Would You Want to Look Like Poo?

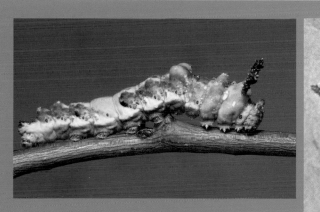

The viceroy (far right) and white admiral (right) caterpillars hide from predators by camouflaging themselves as bird droppings. If you were a bird, would this fake poop fool you?

WHAT'S in a NAME?

Animals get their names for all sorts of unusual reasons. They may be named for the way they look, or because of the way they act. They may be given the name of the first person to discover them, or for where they live.

Cute Fly, Gross Name!

Dung flies are a large group of flies. They do not look like dung! Instead, they earned their name because they are often found in cow pastures. Some types of dung flies lay their eggs in cow patties.

Recycle!

There are more than 35,000 types of dung beetles. These beetles roll dung from plant-eating animals (herbivores) into balls, then roll the dung balls down into underground tunnels. A female dung beetle lays her eggs near the dung balls, giving her offspring fresh food to eat when they hatch. Dung beetles are an important part of many ecosystems because they aerate soil and recycle nutrients.

Never Arm Wrestle a Dung Beetle!

Researchers who measured the strength of one type of dung beetle found males that could pull 1,141 times their own body weight. Biologists believe this makes the dung beetle the world's strongest insect!

TO BURY OR NOT

Our pets may have inherited their bathroom habits from their relatives. Dogs do not bury their feces, perhaps because, like their ancestors, they are pack animals that use chemicals in their feces to talk with other group members. Domestic cats bury their feces, perhaps to hide the chemical cues in their feces that would advertise their presence to predators.

Can Fluffy Be Potty Trained?

Kittens quickly learn from their moms to dig holes in kitty litter or in dirt outdoors. When people want to teach their cats how to use human toilets, it usually takes a lot of practice!

Check out the tiger scat in the photo below. Tiger scat is unusual because some ends have twisting, curving shapes!

Bobcats (left), especially young or nursing females, bury their feces under leaves and soil. Sometimes bobcats make scrapes, the way tigers do. (See below.)

Tiger Scrapes Mark the Spot

Tigers mark their territories with "scrapes." To make a scrape, a tiger pushes dirt up and back with each hind paw, then urinates or defecates on the scrape.

TO BURY?

Who Needs Text Messages?

When cats and dogs defecate, small amounts of fluid in their anal glands are released on top of their feces. This fluid gives information about the pooper's age, gender, health, and reproductive status. When cats and dogs sniff each other's rear ends as a greeting, they are sniffing this same anal gland fluid.

 ## Dogs Scrape, Too!

Skunks are well known for their defensive tricks. To fight off predators, they release their anal gland fluid all at once, drenching their predators in a hard-to-remove layer of stinky liquid!

THE POOP PATROL

It's always been good manners to clean up our pets' fecal remains, but now it's the law in many places. Feces in public places can transmit diseases and attract rats and mice.

Scoop That Poop!

PET WASTE

TRANSMITS DISEASE

LEASH-CURB AND CLEAN UP
AFTER YOUR
PET

IT'S THE LAW
$25.00 TO $200.00 FINE

SCHOOL
CHILDREN PLAY HERE

POOP FREE ZONE!

HORSE OWNERS ARE
RESPONSIBLE FOR
CLEANING UP AFTER
THEIR ANIMALS.

Can't We
Just Blame
The Cat?

Watch Out!

THE LATRINE SCENE

Latrines are specific places animals use for defecating and sometimes also urinating. Badgers (left) dig pits for their latrines, while rhinos (below) leave their poop in big piles that mark their territory. Rhinos often walk through the feces in their latrines, which spreads their group's scent as they walk.

People use latrines, also. At right is an ancient Roman latrine in Ostia Antica, Italy.

More Mammal Latrines

Several other types of mammals also use latrines, including raccoons, foxes, meerkats, and otters (clockwise from top left). Biologists have found that meerkats share their latrines with neighboring groups.

Poop Time Capsules?

Chinchillas (below right) also defecate in latrines. They mix their feces with plants, then urinate on them, which forms crystals that seal the latrine. Biologists in Chile are using chinchilla latrines that are thousands of years old to get information about past weather patterns and habitats.

Living in groups offers many benefits to insects, including protection from the cold and predators, and shared home-building and food-finding. Some insects live in groups only when they are young, as larvae; others, such as termites, bees, and ants, live in groups when young and also as adults. Living as a group can cause some problems, though. If you live in one place and don't have latrines, what happens to all that poo?

Poop-Free Homes

Tent caterpillars (left) defecate through holes in their silk tents! Bees solve their fecal problems in a different way. The larvae of many species do not defecate until they are about to emerge from their egg cells. In other species, adult bees clean out the poop from each cell. Many adult bees "hold" their feces all winter, then defecate when they fly out in the spring.

PLANKTON POO

Plankton contains millions of small, floating plants, animals, seeds, and eggs in fresh and salt waters around the world. Science textbooks talk a lot about the importance of plankton to the world's food chains, but did you know that the feces from these floating animals might be even more important for its role in organic carbon cycling?

When the plankton animals defecate, their fecal pellets fall downward. Eventually, the carbon atoms from their feces can become part of the bodies of animals living in deeper water. How's that for recycling?

Whale feces brings iron to the surface, which increases algae growth, which creates more food for krill, which creates more food for some types of whales and other krill-eaters.

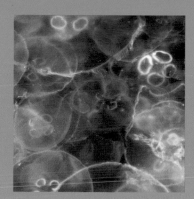

Meet the Floaters

Clockwise from above left, here are just a few examples of animals that are part of plankton: moon jellyfish, fish eggs attached to seaweed, fish larva, rotifer, octopus larva, shrimp larva, and sea slug larva. Scientists who study plankton animal feces can tell which type of animal a pellet came from just by its shape!

Yahoo for Whale Poo!

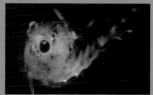

UNDERWATER POO

Hitchhiking Seeds? Thumbs up!

According to new research, the tambaqui fish (below), a seed-eating fish found in the Amazon, may be able to move tree seeds more than 3 miles! This type of dispersal is good for the seeds because when they leave the fish's body through its feces, the seeds may land in a place with less competition for soil and sun, farther away from close relatives.

Cool Food Chains

Ice holes in Antarctic ice caves are good for more than just curious scuba divers. Seal feces falls through the holes, serving as a food source for the sea stars waiting below. The sea stars also release feces, because they are animals. Their feces dissolves over time, feeding smaller animals and moving carbon back into the ecosystem.

UNDERWATER POO

Marine Mud: Wonder What's in There?

Have Fun at Work!

Biologists recently tested the calcium carbonate that makes up the muddy bottoms of tropical sea floors. They found that 14% of this "marine mud" came from fish poop.

If a Little Poo Is Good, Isn't More Poo Even Better?

Although the sea stars on page 49 benefit from seal feces, too much poop can be bad for aquatic habitats. In places where humans raise large numbers of hogs or cows, for example, a lot of feces can run into streams and rivers after rains, bringing with it disease-causing parasites and adding materials that can disrupt ecosystems.

Duckweed, a floating water plant that serves as food for fish and water birds, is able to filter out many of the extra nutrients from hog and cow run-off. Biological engineers studying the filtering ability of duckweed recently discovered that the plant can make biofuel from hog feces.

Who Goes There?

When biologists looked at the shapes of calcium carbonate crystals from several kinds of tropical fish feces under strong microscopes, they found they could identify the feces of these fish in the marine mud, including the snapper fish at left and the barracuda fish above. Each type of fish may have its own unique "fecal print," the same way people have unique fingerprints!

FIGHT OR FLIGHT

"Fight or flight" responses help animals deal with dangerous situations by giving them a burst of extra oxygen and extra sugar, which helps their bodies make energy for fighting or escaping.

Poopy Pets

Ever notice that guinea pigs, mice, gerbils, and hamsters poop a lot when you handle them? Because rodents are preyed upon in the wild by carnivores, they have very sensitive fight or flight responses that can be stimulated by human touch.

Playing 'Possum

When threatened, opossums can "play dead" for hours to fool predators. Sometimes they also release a stinky green anal liquid!

"Don't Mess with Me!"

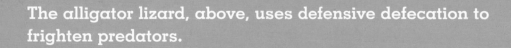

Phrase of the Day

DEFENSIVE DEFECATION: The release of feces by a prey animal to shock or scare away a predator. Some animals use defensive regurgitation (puking!) to frighten predators.

The alligator lizard, above, uses defensive defecation to frighten predators.

Residents of remote Tibet have been using yak dung as their energy source for centuries. Although railroads that can bring in coal have recently been built, many people hope the dung traditions will continue because dung is better for the environment and readily available. The yak dung heap below is drying and will be ready to use soon.

ALL THIS POO?

Yaks (left and below right) are large mammals related to cows and bison. They have been living in Tibet for about 3,000 years and are also found in Russia and central Asia.

Yak Heat!

Yak Stacks!

Burning dried yak dung provides heat in hut homes and around campfires. Stacks of drying dung patties are a common sight on mountain landscapes.

In many parts of India and Pakistan, dried cow dung is used as heating fuel and to make electricity. In some areas of India, Pakistan, and Africa, dried cow dung is also used to line floors and walls to provide heat and repel insects. It can even be polished so it shines!

Cleaner Than Coal!

Like yak dung, cow dung needs to be air-dried before it can be used for energy or home construction. Believe it or not, methane in the dung provides the same type of fuel as the gasoline in your car or the coal that makes electricity to power your home's refrigerator.

ALL THIS POO?

A Dung Stash: Like Money In the Bank!

Below: Wet cow dung can be pressed against walls to dry.

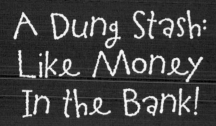

BATHROOM HABITS

There's only one thing you can say for sure about the pooping patterns of animals: Every animal is different, and sometimes the same animal changes behavior when situations change.

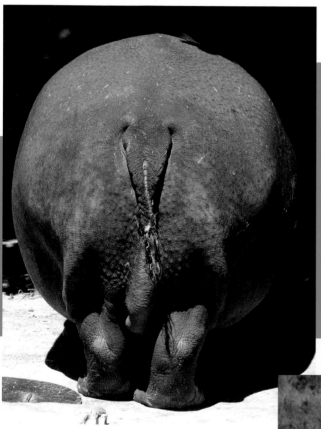

Stand Back!

See the cute little tail on the large hippo at left? To mark their territories, hippos spin their tails around and around when they poop, spraying their feces in all directions!

When a zebra's tail is up, it's either defecating or having its hindquarters groomed by an oxpecker bird. Oxpeckers have similar symbiotic relationships with many large mammals: The bird gets a high-protein meal, and the mammal gets groomed.

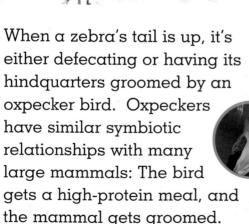

Sloths spend most of their time hanging upside down in trees, even when eating and sleeping! They do not defecate upside down, though. Instead, they crawl down the tree once a week to poop. Biologists do not understand the reasons for this behavior yet.

Feces Outlives Species

Feces from the Shasta ground sloth can still be found in areas of the American Southwest, even though this type of sloth has been extinct for about 13,000 years. The Joshua tree, whose seeds were found in the sloth's dung samples, is at risk of becoming extinct because of temperature increases.

BETTER WITH AGE?

Discovering old animal feces makes some people very happy. WHAT? Did you really just read that? You sure did. Creative people are making jewelry from the poop of reindeer, elephants, and many other animals, and fossil lovers are thrilled to find dinosaur dung in gift shops or on dig sites.

When's Mom's Birthday?

Crafting with Moose Poo

How do you make moose poop pretty enough to wear as jewelry? First, the droppings are dried and sterilized. Next, they are shaped, polished, painted, and placed in jewelry settings. The moose "jewels" can even be sprayed with glitter!

Word of the Day

COPROLITE: *Fossilized feces.*

The word coprolite comes from the Greek words for dung and stone. Coprolites do not smell bad and are prized by dinosaur fossil hunters. The fossilized dung of carnivorous dinosaurs sometimes has the bones of prey animals in it!

Dinosaur Coprolite

No Latrines Here!

In Alaska and Canada's Yukon, people have found areas that are covered in frozen caribou coprolites. The layers of frozen feces are more than 100 feet deep!

WILD & WACKY

The wild and wacky pages that follow will give you just a peek at the amazing ways feces affects competition, reproduction, and everyday life in animals. For example, three-lined potato beetles hide under a thick layer of their feces. The feces has toxins in it because of the plants the beetle eats, and these chemicals repel predators and parasites.

Because we are mammals and our pets are often mammals, it's easy to forget how much protection a mammal's growing embryo receives in the female's uterus. You might say our thinking is a little mammal-centric. Animals that are not mammals go to great effort to protect their growing embryos. Millipedes, for example, make nests from their feces, and then cover their eggs with more feces for extra protection from always-hungry egg predators. Aren't you glad you're a mammal?

Sweet Dreams?

Ever wonder why people with asthma and allergies use plastic covers over their pillows and mattresses? Dust mites often live in our bedding, feeding on the dead skin cells that come off as we sleep. A protein on the frass of dust mites can trigger allergic reactions, and the covers offer protection. The frass of some other insects (including the cockroach shown at left) and some spiders can also cause allergies in people.

Self Defense

The caterpillars of skipper butterflies (right) shoot their poop far away to throw predatory wasps off their trails. The wasps use chemicals in the skippers' feces to find them. Cicadas (above left) poop when threatened by a predator. See page 53 to learn about other animals that do this behavior.

Phrase of the Day: "Flea Dirt"

Flea dirt isn't dirt at all, although it's easy to see why these dirt-like particles earned their common name. Flea dirt is actually flea feces! Grossed out yet? Flea feces contains a lot of dried blood because a female flea eats your pet's blood to nourish her eggs. Don't believe it? Place a little flea dirt in a drop of water and watch it turn red! (If you do this, make sure you wash your hands afterward.)

Don't Kiss an Insect, Even If It's Really Cute!

In South and Central America, an insect known by its common name of kissing bug has transferred the *Trypanosoma cruzi* parasite to more than 16 million people. The parasite causes Chagas disease, which kills about 50,000 people per year. The insect's feces is commonly found in houses with mud floors and walls, and causes infection when it gets in someone's eyes, mouth, or even a bite wound. Look for the parasite in the blood sample above right; the blood cells are purple and the worm-like parasite is magenta.

WILD & WACKY

Some rhymes are just too much fun to resist. When a tree shrew in Borneo was found using a pitcher plant like a toilet bowl, British newspapers ran stories about a shrew loo. A loo, in case you don't know, is a British word for bathroom.

The pitcher plant secretes a sweet liquid around its rim to attract shrews, and the shrew's feces fertilizes the plant!

Herbivores Rock

Many types of fungi live in the feces of herbivores (plant-eating animals). Although mushroom spores could find nutrients in the feces of carnivores (meat-eating animals), they may like herbivore dung more because they don't have to compete with as many bacteria.

Yum, Bones Are Tasty!

Hyena poop does something most other mammal feces does not: It fossilizes well. Any idea why hyena poop might still be around after 200,000 years? Hyenas eat the bones of their prey, unlike many other carnivores, so their feces is filled with calcium, which helps it fossilize.

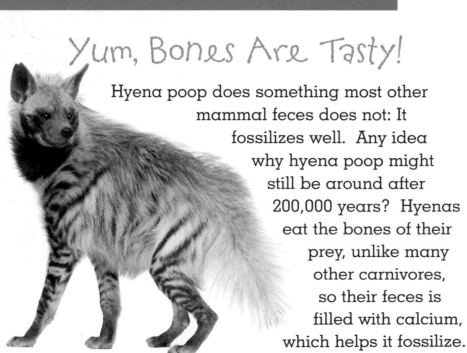

HORSE POO
$2.00 bag

This week only: Buy one bag, get one bag free! How many would you like?

The Best Nest!

Who Stole My Poo?

The secretary bird makes its large nests, which are bigger than a king-size bed, in the tops of trees in Africa. The nest is built from sticks, animal fur, and zebra dung.

Poo Pollution?

Fish farms are a good way to raise food for humans without taking too many fish from their natural habitats. Just like hog farmers, fish farmers have to find ways to get rid of all that poo so they don't pollute rivers and streams.

Cancer-Sniffing Canine Surprises Docs!

Japanese researchers have trained a female black Labrador Retriever to sniff out the presence of colon cancer in the breath and feces of humans.

WILD & WACKY

Colors Give Clues

RIGHT: The Adélie penguins in Antarctica have pink poo when they eat krill (above, right) and brown poo when they eat squid (above, left) or small fish. When groups of birds are feeding on krill, they leave so much pink poo on rocks that the pink color can be seen in satellite photos taken from space! Check out the feces from this penguin and decide what type of food he had for dinner.

BELOW: Conservation biologist Dr. Sam Wasser uses orca whale poop to test for toxins and to sequence DNA. Dr. Wasser says the poop looks like algae mixed with mucus, and that's not the cool part. Ready for how he collects floating whale poop? His poop-sniffing dog, Tucker, finds it for him.

Fetch That Feces!

Birds Have the Last Laugh

Why, Oh Why?

If you're always on the look-out for poison ivy, you may have noticed that the plants are often found growing under electric lines and fences. Do you have any ideas why? Because birds release the seeds in their feces when they're resting on wires and fences.

A Geisha facial contains feces from nightingale birds and promises to make the user's skin look younger. Not to worry, bacteria and parasites are killed before the feces is brushed onto someone's face.

My, You Look Lovely Today

Birds are very careful about where they lay their eggs. The temperature has to be just right, and the eggs have to be hidden from hungry predators.

In Africa, the double-banded courser bird lays its eggs on the ground, next to antelope poop. The courser's eggs have the same color and pattern as the antelope poop, which confuses egg-eating predators.

It's a bird. It's a plane. No, it's a Northern flicker bird removing a fecal sac from its nest! If you can't remember what a fecal sac is, check out the terms on page 10 again.

POOP DETECTIVES

Questions, questions, questions! People who try to identify animals by their feces often use questions such as these to guide them to the correct answer.

1. Is the sample solid and tubular and usually a brown or black color?

Is the sample feces in the shape of small, seed-like shapes? If so, your sample may be from a MOUSE.

Does the sample have a circular or oblong shape? If so, your sample may be from a DEER (oblong with ripples) or from a RABBIT (circular and smooth).

Does the sample have a tubular shape that's **less** than an inch long? If so, your sample may be from a SQUIRREL (rounded at both ends), or from a RAT (irregular ends with rough texture), or from a BAT (flat on one end and pointed on the other and sometimes sparkly from insect exoskeletons).

Does the sample have a tubular shape that's **more** than an inch long? If so, your sample may be from a CAT (tapered and pointed on one end), or from a FOX (tapered at both ends), or from a SKUNK (rough texture, few or no plant parts visible, insect parts visible, usually dark).

2. Is the sample in the form of dried splay or fluid and usually a white or light color?

Has the sample dried to a powder and/or is there a white cap at one end? If so, your sample may be from a REPTILE.

Is the sample fluid or dried liquid with splatter? If so, your sample may be from a BIRD.

POO INTERVIEW

Let's face it: Some jobs involve more poo than others. A video game designer never interacts with feces at work, while veterinarians, like Dr. Beth Snyder, work with feces every day. Here, Dr. Snyder answers some Poo Interview questions.

Can you tell what's wrong with an animal from its poo?

Yes, in some diseases, examining the stool will give us the diagnosis, such as some anemias and gastrointestinal illnesses. Poop is a very useful source of answers concerning an animal's health. We look at the consistency (runny vs. solid), color, odor, frequency, and amount. We also look for abnormal findings such as blood, sticks, mucus, bone fragments, and more. In vet medicine we have to use all our senses. In many cases, the senses of smell (yuck) and sight can help greatly with a diagnosis.

How often do animals defecate in your waiting room?

Numerous times a day. I chalk it up to nerves! It is quickly removed and the floor is mopped every time.

How do you search feces for parasites?

Some intestinal parasites can be seen with the naked eye. We also use fecal flotation tests, where the feces is mixed with a saline solution, and the eggs rise to the top of a fecal analyzer. (A fecal analyzer is a fancy term for a small plastic tube that the poop is mixed in.) We place a slide on the surface of the poop and then examine it under a microscope.

Which poop question do pet owners ask most often?

Why does my dog eat its own poop or the poop of other animals? People also want to know if their dog has worms when it scoots its butt across the floor. It's not likely; the dog's anal glands are probably full.

LEARN MORE . . .

This book could easily have been 800 or even 8,000 pages long and there would still be hundreds of cool examples of animal poop. Check out these ideas to continue your learning fun.

Word Games . . .

Look up the etymology (word history) of your favorite fecal terms on page 10. Which ones surprised you the most? Research the scat fish shown here. Where did its name come from?

Cruise the Web

Pick an animal, any animal, then do a Web search on that animal to discover information about that animal and its body waste. Is the feces used for communication? Defense? Does it use latrines or dig holes? Does it eat feces or lay eggs in it? Any animal you choose is guaranteed to have a great feces story associated with it. If you don't find fabulous info on the first try, keep looking!

Get out Your Calculator

Choose a place where there are lots of animals: a zoo, an aquarium, a city park, or your backyard. First make a list of all the animals that live there. Then add up how many of each type of animal live there. Then look up how many times and how much each of those animals defecates every day. Why, oh why, don't you see poop everywhere?

Think It Through

What do you think the poop of amphibians such as frogs and salamanders looks like? Hint: They have one opening for both solid and liquid waste, called a cloaca, the way birds and reptiles do because they are more closely related to those types of animals than they are to placental mammals, like us.

Scavenger Hunt: Find Those Worm Castings!

Worm castings look like piles of worms, but are really fecal material. Look for them anywhere there is soil or sand. You might even be able to sell your treasures because organic gardeners purchase worm castings to fertilize their plants.

Check It Out

Observant kids have noticed a few unusual things about the foods they eat and their next-day poop. Corn on the cob may taste yummy, but our bodies can only digest the outer coating of the corn seeds; the rest of the kernel comes out in our feces. And what happens when you eat blue ice cream or other foods with dyes? You don't know? Give it a try in the name of science. And what happens if you eat a lot of fatty foods? Or high-fiber foods? (Hints: floating and sinking!)

GLOSSARY

ABIOTIC: Something that is not alive. Rocks and rain clouds are abiotic parts of habitats.

BACTERIA: Single-celled organisms that do not have membranes around specialized areas in their cells.

BIOTIC: Something that is alive. Examples include bacteria, fungi, animals, and plants.

CARNIVORE: An animal or plant that eats animals. Examples include tigers, wolves, starfish, seals, sharks, crocodiles, and Venus fly traps.

CLOACA: The single opening found in amphibians, birds, reptiles, and the monotreme mammals through which both feces and urine waste products leave the bodies. The cloaca is also used for releasing gametes (sperm and egg cells).

DIGESTIVE SYSTEM: The parts of an animal's body responsible for breaking down food into small, usable parts and for getting rid of usable parts as waste.

ECOSYSTEM: The living and nonliving parts of an environment that function together as a group.

FORAGING: An animal's process of searching for food. Foraging takes energy and sometimes puts the forager at risk of being found by a predator.

HABITAT: The home for an organism or a group of organisms.

HERBIVORE: An animal that eats plants. Examples include rabbits and zebras.

PREDATOR: An animal searching for organisms to eat.

READ MORE

Because You Care Deeply about Animals, Ecosystems, and the Environment . . .

Jurassic Poop: What Dinosaurs (and Others) Left Behind written by Jacob Berkowitz and illustrated by Steve Mack; Kids Can Press (2006).

Scats and Tracks of North America: A Field Guide to the Signs of Nearly 150 Wildlife Species (Scats and Tracks Series) written by James Halfpenny and illustrated by Todd Telander; Falcon (2008).

What Shat That?: A Pocket Guide to Poop Identity by Matt Pagett; Ten Speed Press (2007).

Zooplankton Fecal Pellet Guide by Dr. Juanita Urban-Rich and colleagues; online at http://www.zfpguide.com.

For Giggles . . .

Everybody Poops 410 Pounds a Year: An Illustrated Bathroom Companion for Grown-Ups written by Deuce Flanagan and illustrated by David R. Dudley; Ulysses Press (2010).

Poop: A Natural History of the Unmentionable written by Nicola Davies and Illustrated by Neal Layton; Candlewick (2011, reprint edition).

The Truth About Poop by Susan E. Goodman; Puffin (2007).

What's Your Poo Telling You? by Anish Sheth, M.D. and Josh Richman; Chronicle Books (2007).

SUBJECT INDEX

Left: Large group of
butterflies feasting on
cow feces.

ORGANISM INDEX

ACKNOWLEDGMENTS

Information from the following individuals, places, and organizations contributed greatly to this book: Dr. Jill T. Anderson, Arizona Museum of Natural History, David Attenborough, Australian Geographic, BBC News, Dr. Karin Beaumont, Dr. G. Boiteau, British Antarctic Survey, Center for Conservation Biology/University of Washington, Centers for Disease Control and Prevention, Dr. Jay Cheng, Dr. Ken Cole, Dr. Jim Costa, www.China.org, Stephen F. Crowley, Dr. Torben Dabelsteen, Dr. Safi K. Darden, Dr. Lisa Dilling, Doñana Biological Station, Duke University, Dr. Richard Despard Estes, Dr. Tim Forrest, Friends of the Australian National Botanic Gardens, Dr. George Galileos, Dr. Debbie Hadley, Dr. Alastair R. Harborneb, Harvard University, Dr. Claudio Latorre Hidalgo, Dr. David Hughes, International Yak Association, Dr. Steve Jackson, Der. Howard L. Jelks, Dr. Pedro Jordano, Dr. J. Kimpinski, Dr. Rob Knell, Kyushu University, Rick Lockamy, Dr. Heino Lepp, Dr. Donald Lewis, Massimo Marcone, National Geographic, National Institute of Health, National Public Radio (NPR), Natural Resources Program/Haywood Community College, Dr. Juan Negro, Dr. Stephen Nicol, North Carolina State University, Opossum Society of the United States, Oregon Public Broadcasting, Dr. Chris T. Perrya, Dr. Jim Petranka, San Diego Zoo, Michael A. Saltera, Dr. Leigh Simmons, Dr. Hideto Sonoda,

Dr. Lise K. Steffensen, Dr. J.G. Stewart, Suburban Tiger Project, Dr. Juanita Urban-Rich, University of Massachusetts-Boston, University of Tasmania/Australian Antarctic Division, Dr. Stephen Vantassel/Internet Center for Wildlife Damage Management (http://icwdm.org/inspection/Scat.aspx), Dr. Mathias Vuille, Dr. Ajai Vyas, Dr. Martha Weiss, Dr. Rod W. Wilson, www.badgers.org/uk, and the Zooplankton Fecal Pellet Guide.

Gratitude is extended to the following photographers and photographic sources for their creative contributions: Aerogondo2, Alslutsky, Anat-Oli, Ilya Andriyanov, Arteki, Abraham Badenhorst, Stacy Barnett, Benedictus, Dean Bertoncelj, Peter Betts, Borislav Borisov, Bork, Mark Bridger, Bonaire 2008/NOAA, Sylvie Bouchard, Yuriy Boyko, Steve Brigman, Brzostowska, David Cappaert/Michigan State University/Bugwood.org, CDC/Dr. Ewan Chesser, Hung Chung Chih, Chromographs, Matthew Cole, Willee Cole, D. P. Photography, Ross Dailey, Graeme Dawes, Gaetano De Blasio, Doglikehorse, EcoPrint, Björn Erlandsson, Melinda Fawver, Fivepointsix, Susan Flashman, Barry Forbes, Four Oaks, Tyler Fox, Fritz16, Frog Traveller, Juan Gaertner, Kevin Giszewski, Maria Gioberti, Igor Golovniov, Sergey Goruppa, Jamie Hall/NOAA, Happystock, Damian Herde, Adrian Hillman, Holbox, Mau Horng, Danylchenko Iaroslav, Iraidka, Eric Isselée, iStockphoto, Tatiana Ivkovich, Marcel Jancovic, Alan Jeffery, Stephan Jezek, Donald M. Jones/Minden Pictures, Joseph Scott Photography, K&D Foster Photographers, Anan Kaewkhammul, Sebastian Kaulitzki, Nickolay Khoroshkov, Vita Khorzhevska, Falk Kienas, Kirsanov, Michael Klenetsky, Devin Koob, Vladimirs Koskins, Grigory Kubatyan, K. Kucharska, D. Kucharski, Andrey Kudinov, David Lade, Ladynin, Erik Lam, Lana Langlois, M. Lorenz, Henrik Larsson, Ch'ien Lee/Minden Pictures, Leksele, Eric Lemar, Carsten Medom Madsen, Cosmin Manci, Jerry Mclelland/NOAA/Charleston Bump Expedition, Shannon Matteson, Dmitry Melnikov, Martina I. Meyer, Mae Melvin, Jason Mintzer, Natursports, NOAA Image Library, Khoroshunova Olga, Tyler Olson, Michael Papasidero, Perutskyi Petro, Kevin Phillips, PhotoEuphoria, Picsfive, Picturepartners, Fritz Polking/FLPA/Minden Pictures, Paul Prescott, Daniel Prudek, Dr. Morley Read, Stéphan Reebs, Bernhard Richter, Ivaschenko Roman, Manz Russali, Marcelo Saavedra, Oleksii Sagitov, Scarabaeus, Becky Sheridan, Shutterstock, Nelson Sirlin, Skynavin, Dr. Carolina K. Smith, South 12th Photography, Becky Stares, Steffen Foerster Photography, Villiers Steyn, Allen Stoner, Tino Strauss/Wikimedia Commons, Nick Stubbs, Anna Subbotina, Johan Swanepoel, Sydeen, Jens Teichmann, Jef Thompson, Tom Tietz, Mike Truchon, Ultrashock, Jiri Vaclavek, Andre Valadao, Rudi Vandeputte, Vilmos Varga, Vishnevskiy Vasily, Valeriy Velikov, Valua Vitaly, Aaron Welch, Darren Whitt, Matt Wilson/Jay Clark, NOAA, World's Wildlife Wonders, Henry Wrenn, Norbert Wu/Minden Pictures, Wxorzist, Pan Xunbin, Steshkin Yevgeniy, Gary Yim, and Zen Garden.

The End!